JUL '08

Backyard Bugs

Chirp, Chirp!

Crickets in Your Backyard

by Nancy Loewen ~ illustrated by Rick Peterson

Thanks to our advisers for their expertise, research, knowledge, and advice:

Blake Newton, Extension Entomologist
University of Kentucky

Susan Kesselring, M.A., Literacy Educator
Rosemount–Apple Valley–Eagan (Minnesota) School District

PICTURE WINDOW BOOKS
Minneapolis, Minnesota

Editorial Director: Carol Jones
Managing Editor: Catherine Neitge
Creative Director: Keith Griffin
Editor: Jill Kalz
Story Consultant: Terry Flaherty
Designer: Nathan Gassman
Page Production: Picture Window Books
The illustrations in this book were created with acrylics.

Picture Window Books
5115 Excelsior Boulevard
Suite 232
Minneapolis, MN 55416
877-845-8392
www.picturewindowbooks.com

Printed in the United States of America.

Library of Congress Cataloging-in-Publication Data
Loewen, Nancy, 1964–
Chirp, chirp! : crickets in your backyard / by Nancy Loewen ; illustrated by Rick Peterson.
p. cm. — (Backyard bugs)
Includes index.
ISBN 1-4048-1141-9 (hardcover)
1. Crickets—Juvenile literature. I. Peterson, Rick, ill. II. Title.
QL508.G8L4 2005
595.7'26—dc22
                                                    2005004057

Table of Contents

Evening Singers

Cree-ee ... cree-ee ... cree-ee ...

What's that chirping sound? It seems to be coming from that bush over there.

cree-ee

Now the sound has stopped. But look! Do you see that brown bug tucked inside the bush? It's a field cricket. It was making all the noise.

Let's catch it and take a closer look.

Field crickets are one of the most common kinds of crickets in the United States. They live in fields, grasslands, or woods, where they hide in moist areas beneath rocks or lumps of dirt.

The Cricket's Body

The cricket looks a lot like a grasshopper. It has big eyes and big hind legs. It can jump up to 20 times the length of its body. And look at its long antennae!

Crickets hear with special body parts on their front legs. They breathe through tiny holes in their abdomens.

9

Crickets have wings, but most of the time they'd rather jump than fly. The male crickets put their wings to a different use—chirping!

Male crickets lift their wings and rub them together to make a song. They are calling for female crickets, telling them it's time to mate.

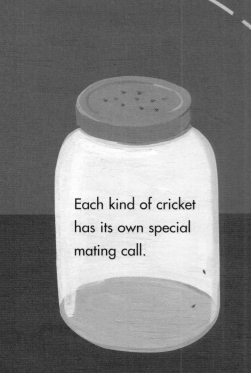

Each kind of cricket has its own special mating call.

Waiting to Hatch

After mating in late summer, the female cricket lays eggs. She has a long, pointed body part, called an ovipositor, at the end of her abdomen. The eggs pass through the ovipositor and are placed directly into the dirt.

Female field crickets lay between 150 and 400 eggs. The eggs are laid one by one rather than in groups.

13

The eggs take a long time to hatch. Fall turns into winter, and winter turns into spring. Finally, when the ground warms up and plants begin to grow, the eggs hatch.

Tiny crickets come out of the dirt. They look just like the adult crickets, but they don't have wings. They are called nymphs.

In cold areas of the world, adult crickets die in fall. Even in warm areas, most crickets don't live for more than one year.

Eating and Growing

The nymphs eat just about any kind of food, including leaves, roots, dead bugs, and rotting fruit. A cricket that gets into a house might even eat cloth or paper.

As a young cricket grows, it sheds its outer shell many times. This process is called molting. After molting 8 to 10 times, a nymph becomes an adult.

Like all bugs, crickets have hard outer shells called exoskeletons. The exoskeleton is what a cricket sheds when it molts.

Crickets have to watch out for many predators. Spiders, birds, frogs, snakes, and lizards eat crickets.

Even larger animals like foxes and raccoons will eat crickets—if they're quick enough to catch a cricket before it jumps away.

Crickets are nocturnal, which means they are most active at night. They avoid many of their enemies by hiding during the day.

19

A Cricket Concert

Listen … It's a cricket concert out there! The males are trying to find females to mate with so that more crickets will sing next summer.

cree-ee

e-ee

Let's put this fellow back where we found him so he can continue his song.

cree-ee

Look Closely at a Cricket

Look at a female field cricket through a magnifying glass. How many of these different parts can you see?

- A cricket uses its **antennae** to touch and smell.

- Four **front legs** are for walking.

- Two **back legs** are for jumping.

- A female cricket has **wings** but doesn't chirp.

- Eggs come out of the long **ovipositor**.

head

thorax

abdomen

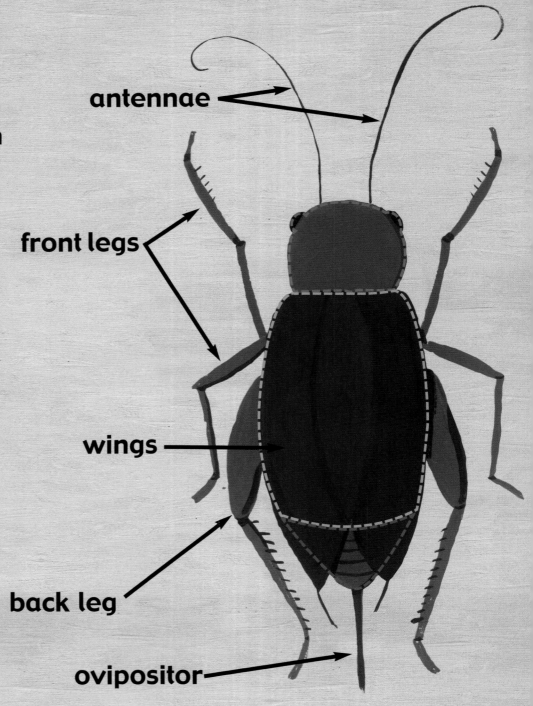

antennae

front legs

wings

back leg

ovipositor

Fun Facts

- Worldwide, there are more than 20,000 kinds of crickets, grasshoppers, katydids, and their relatives.

- The warmer it is, the faster crickets chirp. Some people say you can tell the temperature by listening to crickets. Count the number of chirps a cricket makes during a 15-second period. Now add 40. The total should be close to the temperature in Fahrenheit degrees.

- For centuries, people in Asia have kept crickets as pets. A cricket in your house is said to bring good luck.

- Grasshoppers sing in the same way that crickets do. But they are active during the day, not at night.

Keeping Crickets

Do you want to learn more about crickets? Watching them up close is the best way.

Look for crickets in damp, sheltered places, such as under rocks or logs. Put them in a clear glass or plastic container. Make sure that air can get in, but the crickets can't get out. Add an egg carton or empty toilet paper roll to provide a hiding place.

Feeding crickets is easy because they eat a lot of things. Dry oatmeal, bran cereal, lettuce, and apple peels are some good food choices. For moisture, put in a piece of orange or a bit of sponge soaked in water. Clean out the cage regularly.

What can you learn about your crickets? How do they change? Be sure to put them back outside after you're done watching them.

Words to Know

abdomen – The abdomen is the last section of a bug's body.

antennae – Antennae (an-TEN-ee) are feelers on a bug's head. They are used for touching and smelling. "Antennae" is the word for more than one antenna (an-TEN-uh).

mate – Male and female crickets mate by joining together special parts of their bodies. After they've mated, the female cricket can lay eggs.

nymphs – When crickets are changing from eggs to adults, they are called nymphs (NIMFS).

ovipositor – The ovipositor is a long, pointed body part on a female cricket through which eggs pass.

predators – Predators are animals that hunt other animals for food.

To Learn More

At the Library

Jacobs, Liza. *Crickets*. San Diego: Blackbirch Press, 2003.

Miller, Heather. *Cricket*. San Diego: Kidhaven Press, 2004.

Squire, Ann O. *Crickets and Grasshoppers*. New York: Children's Press, 2003.

On the Web

FactHound offers a safe, fun way to find Web sites related to this book. All of the sites on FactHound have been researched by our staff. *www.facthound.com*

1. Visit the FactHound home page.
2. Enter a search word related to this book, or type in this special code: 1404811419.
3. Click on the FETCH IT button.

Your trusty FactHound will fetch the best sites for you!

Look for all of the books in the Backyard Bugs series:

Busy Buzzers: Bees in Your Backyard

Bzzz, Bzzz! Mosquitoes in Your Backyard

Chirp, Chirp! Crickets in Your Backyard

Dancing Dragons: Dragonflies in Your Backyard

Flying Colors: Butterflies in Your Backyard

Garden Wigglers: Earthworms in Your Backyard

Hungry Hoppers: Grasshoppers in Your Backyard

Living Lights: Fireflies in Your Backyard

Night Fliers: Moths in Your Backyard

Spotted Beetles: Ladybugs in Your Backyard

Tiny Workers: Ants in Your Backyard

Weaving Wonders: Spiders in Your Backyard

Index